FERRY

TRAVEL

GUIDES

What's That Island?

POINTS OF INTEREST, HISTORY AND WILDLIFE
ON THE BC FERRIES ROUTE BETWEEN
SWARTZ BAY AND TSAWWASSEN
(VICTORIA – VANCOUVER)

BRUCE WHITTINGTON

Stray Feathers Press

Whether this is your first trip or your hundredth crossing aboard BC Ferries on the spectacular trip between Vancouver Island and the Lower Mainland, you will find yourself asking, "What's that island? Why are those birds here? What's that lighthouse?" This guide will help you answer many of those questions.

Using The Guide

This map shows you how the guide is organized. If you are travelling from Vancouver and hence sailing from Tsawwassen, start on page 4 and work from there to the back of the book. If you are coming from Victoria and sailing from Swartz Bay, start on page 16 and work toward the front of the book.

Follow your route along each map as the ferry makes its one hour and thirty-five minute crossing and learn more about the area by reading the information on the map, the adjacent page, or at the end of the guide. If you are exploring some of the islands on one of the smaller ferries, these routes are also indicated on the maps.

You can watch the scenery unfold from the comfort of the lounges, but you will see more if you spend time on the outer decks. Be aware that the ship's horn may sound unexpectedly, and it is very loud. The ship's crew will sometimes announce wildlife sightings over the public address system. When trying to find the right side of the ship, remember that the port side is the left side (both have four letters), and the starboard is the right side.

There is more information about the natural history of the Gulf Islands on pages 18 through 24.

This is the first in a series of Ferry Travel Guides. To learn about other guides, please visit the Stray Feathers Press web site: www.strayfeathers.ca.

Salt Spring Island is the largest of the Canadian Gulf Islands, and the only one with sizeable lakes. Galiano Island lies across Trincomali Channel on the far right.

Ups and Downs

ISLAND GEMS IN THE SALISH SEA

You are travelling through a unique archipelago, a collection of islands that hosts a diversity of plants, animals and people that is unparalleled in Canada. The British Columbia coast is marked with rugged mountain ranges and steep valleys. The slopes do not stop when they reach the sea, and ocean depths in the southern Strait of Georgia reach 200 metres, with depths up to 730 metres at Jervis Inlet.

The Strait of Georgia — known by many as the Salish Sea — is home to the Canadian Gulf Islands and the San Juan Islands in the U.S. These islands are mostly formed of sedimentary rocks laid down after the underlying rock was pushed to this coast over hundreds of millions of years. The sedimentary rock has been folded, and the softer layers of sandstone have eroded more quickly, leaving a pattern of long narrow islands, inlets and channels. There are also isolated outcrops of older volcanic rocks on southern Salt Spring, western Portland, and Moresby Islands. The land has been dramatically altered by at least three glaciations, the last receding about 13,000 years ago.

CHANGEABLE WEATHER

The south coast of British Columbia is not so affectionately known as the "Wet Coast," but in fact the climate can vary significantly over a short distance. Victoria lies in the rain shadow of the Olympic Mountains of Washington and as a result receives an annual precipitation of about 600 mm. Across the Strait of Georgia in White Rock, the average annual precipitation is about 1,100 mm, and if you cross the Lion's Gate Bridge to the mountains on the north shore of Vancouver, you can expect about 2,000 mm of precipitation a year. These rain-soaked mountains support some of the largest and oldest Yellow Cedars in British Columbia, in sharp contrast to some of the Salish Sea's rocky promontories and islets, where you can find Brittle Prickly-Pear Cactus in bloom in the summer.

FIRST PEOPLES

First Nations people have lived in British Columbia for thousands of years, with archaeological finds dating to about 9,000 years ago on the coast, and occupation much earlier than that according to oral tradition. Recent research suggests that the first humans to return after the retreat of the ice may have come south along the West Coast, rather than from the interior of North America as was previously thought.

The First Nations of the south coast of British Columbia are Coast Salish, and they share many cultural and linguistic similarities. There are 19 different First Nations that have expressed a historical interest in the southern Gulf Islands area. The Halkomelem people live in several communities on the mainland, central Vancouver Island, and some of the smaller Gulf Islands. They speak a language known as Hul'qumi'num. The second major group is the Northern Straits people, comprising several nations on southern Vancouver Island, the Gulf Islands, and in nearby Washington. Their language is called SENCOTEN. All of these communities traditionally used the Gulf Islands for settlements, food-gathering and hunting. Their names for these sites often reflect their importance. Prevost Island is known in the Hul'qumi'num dialect as Hwu'eshwum, and in the SENCOTEN dialect as WÁWEN, but both refer to the seals that were hunted there.

This photograph by Francis George Claudet shows four people " . . . believed to be of the Chawassen or Salish tribe." IMAGE E-06423 COURTESY OF ROYAL BC MUSEUM, BC ARCHIVES

The extremes of rainfall on the West Coast produce a rich diversity of plants from the Brittle Prickly-Pear Cactus (above) to the Yellow Cedar (below.)

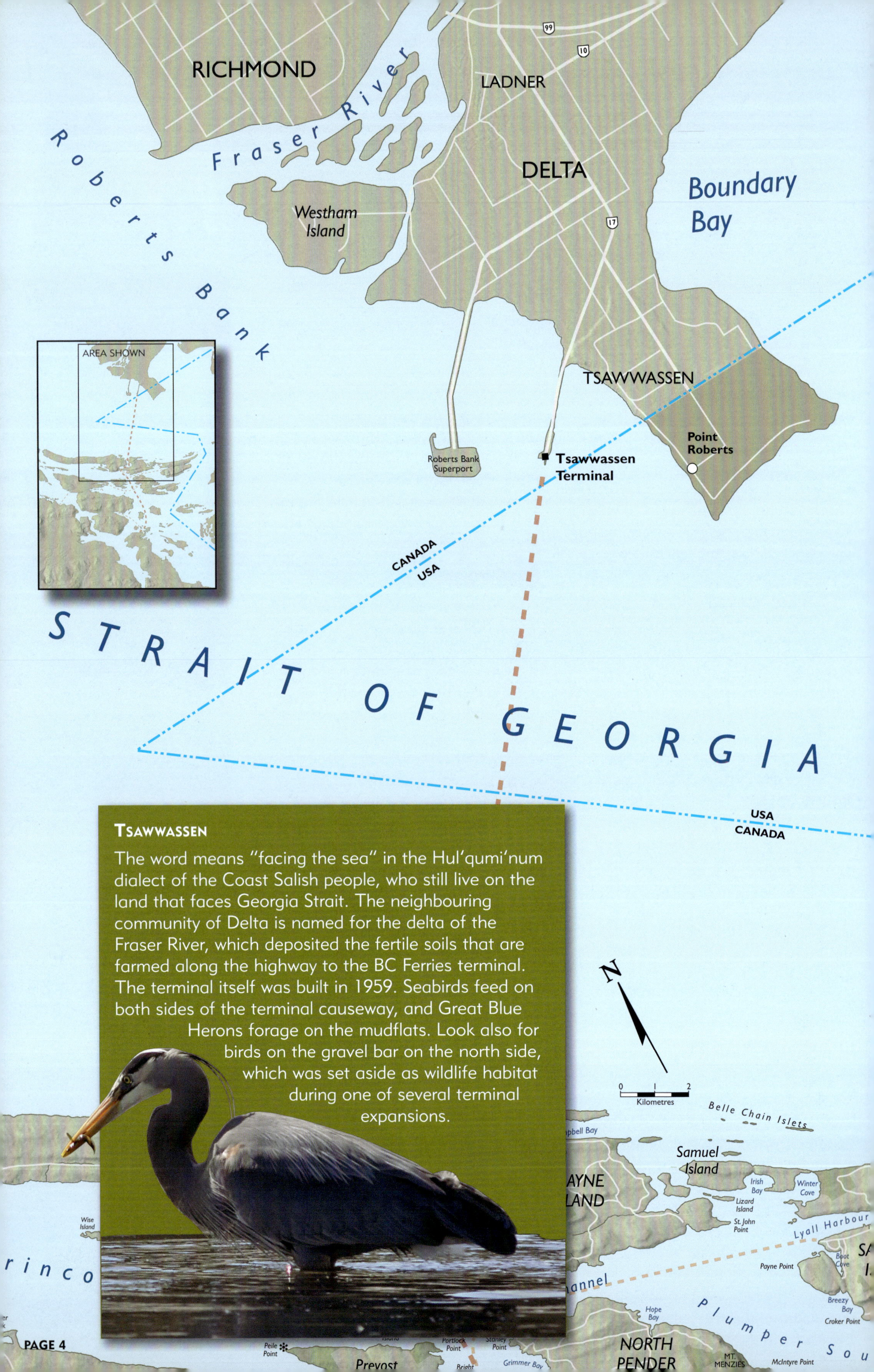

TSAWWASSEN

The word means "facing the sea" in the Hul'qumi'num dialect of the Coast Salish people, who still live on the land that faces Georgia Strait. The neighbouring community of Delta is named for the delta of the Fraser River, which deposited the fertile soils that are farmed along the highway to the BC Ferries terminal. The terminal itself was built in 1959. Seabirds feed on both sides of the terminal causeway, and Great Blue Herons forage on the mudflats. Look also for birds on the gravel bar on the north side, which was set aside as wildlife habitat during one of several terminal expansions.

Roberts Bank Superport at dusk

LEGACY OF A MIGHTY RIVER

FRASER RIVER

The Fraser River rises 1,400 kilometres away in the northern Rocky Mountains. It is British Columbia's largest river, draining a basin of more than 231,000 square kilometres — about a quarter of the province. The broad river enters the Strait of Georgia just south of Vancouver and leaves a plume of sediment-laden fresh water floating on top of the denser sea water.

ROBERTS BANK SUPERPORT

The coal port at Roberts Bank was constructed in 1970 to handle the export of coal from southeastern British Columbia to Asia. Ships up to 260,000 tonnes load 21 million tonnes of coal and coke a year. Two berths were added for container ships in 1987 and handle over half a million containers a year.

BOUNDARY BAY

At one time, the great river entered the sea at what is now Boundary Bay, but as sediment built up there, the river changed direction. The Fraser estuary, including Boundary Bay, is an important wintering and migrating area for waterfowl, shorebirds and birds of prey, and is part of the Western Hemisphere Shorebird Reserve Network.

DRAWING THE LINE

The international boundary was nominally set in 1842 at the 49th parallel, but there was confusion about how the line divided the US and Canadian Gulf Islands. Tension led to the shooting of a British pig on San Juan Island, an event that prompted a heightened military presence there. Discretion prevailed for some years, and the pig remained the only casualty of the "Pig War." The border question was finally resolved in 1872 by a third party — the German emperor, who was Queen Victoria's grandson. Today, BC Ferries traffic between Active Pass and Tsawwassen passes through a small wedge of American waters. Residents of Point Roberts are isolated from the rest of their American compatriots.

Fraser River plume

COURTESY GALIANO CONSERVANCY ASSOCIATION

British Columbia is home to five species of Pacific salmon: Chinook, Chum, Coho, Pink and Sockeye. Although each of the five species has a slightly different life cycle, the basic story is much the same. The young salmon spend the first part of their lives in the streams where they hatched, moving to salt water some months later. They spend a period of one to several years growing to adulthood in the food-rich waters of the Pacific Ocean. At some unknown signal, they are called back to the streams where they were born.

Their voyage home is nothing less than epic, travelling across thousands of kilometres of ocean. Guided possibly by electromagnetic fields and later by "smell," they return to their natal streams, some along the coast, and some far inland along major river systems. With bodies brightly coloured and distorted in preparation for spawning, they battle their way past riffles and chutes until they arrive at a familiar stretch of riverbed.

Males fight for the right to fertilize the eggs laid by the females, which use their tails to dig nests called redds in the gravel in preparation for egg-laying. When spawning is finished, the exhausted fish die and their carcasses attract other wildlife. The nutrients of the dying salmon are recycled into the streamside forests, to shade the waters for the next generation of salmon.

Active Pass

The transit of Active Pass is a highlight of the journey between Tsawwassen and Swartz Bay, but it has not always been this way. The twists and turns were avoided by sailing ships as too treacherous. The name "Active" does not come from the strong tidal currents and heavy marine traffic in the pass, but from American Lieutenant Commander James Alden's steam-powered survey ship *Active*. The British Captain G.H. Richards unknowingly named the pass after his ship, HMS *Plumper*, but politely deferred to the American name. Locals continued to use the British name, and the post office on Mayne Island was called Plumper Pass until 1900.

The Active Pass light on Georgina Point, Mayne Island, with Mount Baker, Washington State in the background

MAYNE ISLAND – GEORGINA POINT: A DANGEROUS COAST

Georgina Shoals off Georgina Point at the northern tip of Mayne Island are typical of the hazards that face mariners on this coast. In 1872, they claimed the three-masted bark *Zephyr*, loaded with 450 tonnes of sandstone columns and blocks to be used in the construction of the San Francisco mint. Her captain and a deckhand were lost in the accident. It was not until 1885 that the picturesque Active Pass light on Georgina Point went into service. The Underwater Archaeology Society of BC located the site of the wreck, and raised two columns and several blocks of sandstone. In 1987, one of the columns, 1.2 metres in diameter and nine metres long, was placed at Newcastle Island Provincial Marine Park near Nanaimo, where the stone was originally quarried.

MAYNE ISLAND – MINERS BAY: THE LURE OF GOLD

Gold in the gravel bars of the Fraser River started a gold rush in 1858, and hopeful miners journeyed to Fort Victoria to embark for the goldfields. Many rowed in open boats to the mouth of the Fraser River. Active Pass was the halfway point of the crossing, and the prospectors camped overnight in the protected bay on Mayne Island now called Miners Bay. Before the Europeans stopped here, the Tsartlip people camped to wait for favourable tides on what is now called Helen Point, on the south side of Active Pass.

▼ This painting by William Bygrave is the only known image of the bark *Zephyr*.
COURTESY THE MARINERS' MUSEUM, NEWPORT NEWS, VA.

Pacific Loons often gather in flocks to feed in the narrow channels among the Gulf Islands.

A Sea Route for Centuries

For thousands of years, people and goods have travelled these waters. In the beginning, large, seaworthy dugout canoes were used. European ships appeared in the eighteenth century, and over the next hundred years, commercial interests provided service to the islands in steamships. In an effort to improve the reliability of service, the provincial government formed BC Ferries. Two ships were launched in 1960 and the fleet has grown dramatically. Today there are 36 vessels serving 47 ports, carrying over 8.5 million vehicles and almost 22 million passengers in 2008.

The steamship *Cy Peck* served the islands as early as 1918 and was bought for relief use by BC Ferries in 1961. Cy Peck was a former Gulf Islands politician and Victoria Cross recipient. SALT SPRING ISLAND ARCHIVES

This view looking southwest from Mount Warburton Pike on Saturna Island shows South Pender Island in the foreground with Moresby and Portland Islands beyond to the left, North Pender just visible on the right, and Salt Spring rising in the distance.

THE EASTERN ISLANDS

SATURNA ISLAND

This is the most removed of the larger Gulf Islands, with a more laid-back pace that reflects the less-frequent ferry service. Because Saturna Island is not as developed, about 40 per cent of the island was acquired as part of the Gulf Islands National Park Reserve. The island was named for the *Santa Saturnina*, a small ship of the Spanish officer José Maria Narvaez, who explored these waters in 1791. Plumper Sound was named decades later for the British survey ship of that name. The name of the Plumper's surgeon is remembered in the name of the bay where the ferry docks — Lyall Harbour. These were not the first people to recognize a safe harbour. The Hul'qumi'num name for the place is Tl'uqayum, which means "calm waters."

Saturna is rugged, rising steeply on its southern shore to its tallest point, the 432 metre summit of Mount Warburton Pike, named after an early white settler.

PENDER ISLANDS

North and South Pender Islands were at one time joined by a small isthmus that was breached in 1911 with the construction of the Pender Canal. This is also the site of one of the oldest First Nations' villages. In the Hul'qumi'num language it was called Tl'e'ulthw ("permanent houses"), and it was occupied as long as 6,000 years ago. The waters were charted in the mid-nineteenth century by Captain Daniel Pender of the Royal Navy, and the islands were named for him. The two Penders are the second most populous of the Gulf Islands, and some islanders commute by ferry to Victoria and Vancouver to work.

The Active Pass Indian Reserve on Mayne Island, photographed in 1935

PREVOST ISLAND

You will not be able to take the ferry to Prevost Island — it is the largest of the Canadian Gulf Islands with no ferry service. It is mostly privately owned, but there are several sites of the Gulf Islands National Park Reserve accessible to kayakers. The Channel Islands between Prevost and Salt Spring Islands are an important sea lion haulout.

Mount Galiano on the right and Helen Point, Mayne Island, on the left mark the southern end of Active Pass.

THE WESTERN ISLANDS

GALIANO ISLAND

The photo at the top of the page is taken near the middle of Active Pass, looking northwest. Mount Galiano, on Galiano Island, is visible at the southern (western) entrance to Active Pass. At 314 metres, it is the highest point on the island. Both are named for Dionisio Alcala Galiano, a Spaniard who explored the region in 1792. In the right foreground is Matthews Point, and on the left is Helen Point on Mayne Island. Galiano Island is typical of the long narrow landforms in the Gulf Islands, stretching 25.3 kilometres from here to Porlier Pass at its northern end, yet it spans less than five kilometres at its widest point.

◀ PREVOST ISLAND

The Portlock Point light on Prevost Island was built in 1896. It had a troubled history, with keepers coming and going at regular intervals. In 1914, the keeper earned $550 a year and was required to work every day of the year. In order to take time off, he had to recruit and pay his own relief. In 1964, the lightkeeper was killed when the house exploded in flames. The light has been automated since 1969.

▲ Harbour Seal

▼ These young Steller's Sea Lions are curious and playful but as adults they will spend more time establishing a place in the hierarchy of the herd.

FLIPPERS FOR FEET

Harbour Seals and Steller's and California Sea Lions are called pinnipeds, which means "fin-feet." All are efficient hunters but must in turn watch for transient Killer Whales, their main predators.

The Harbour Seal is the mammal most likely seen by visitors to coastal British Columbia. They are completely at home in the water, but on land they are quite comical. Their streamlined bodies lie on exposed rocks like great perogies, touching the ground only at their midsections. Unlike sea lions, seals cannot move on land using their flippers, so they do a sort of a hop-flop to get back to the water.

Two species of sea lions occur in BC waters. Sea lions gather at "haul-outs," where the two species may loaf side-by-side. They are sometimes seen on the rocks in Active Pass. The Steller's Sea Lion breeds along the West Coast from California north to Alaska's Aleutian Archipelago. The male, or bull, is a huge animal, with an average weight of about 700 kilograms. The females are a third as large. Steller's Sea Lion numbers are declining.

California Sea Lions breed to the south of British Columbia, and after the breeding season, the bulls disperse. Many move as far north as BC. Bulls of this species can be distinguished from the Steller's by their darker pelts, which look black when wet, and by the prominently ridged foreheads. Bulls weigh up to 350 kilograms. This playful species is well known as the trained circus "seal." The population is increasing, following decades of harvesting for meat and oil.

SALT SPRING ISLAND: THE MELTING POT

Salt Spring Island was home to First Nations as early as 5,000 years ago. With the arrival of Europeans, this largest of the Gulf Islands drew new settlers. In addition to white Europeans, blacks from the United States sought new lives here. The Hudson Bay Company drew on the British links to Hawaii, bringing immigrant workers called Kanakas. Later, Japanese settlers arrived. Many of today's islanders are descended from these early residents, and are joined by an eclectic influx of artists, musicians, and retirees.

Baynes Peak in Mount Maxwell Provincial Park rises behind Fulford Harbour as a ferry approaches.

EASTERN SALT SPRING

Legally, the name is "Saltspring," but locals prefer two words. Either way, it is a tribute to the salty pools on the north end of the island. This is the largest of the Gulf Islands, and boasts the highest mountain as well — the 709-metre Bruce Peak. There is abundant evidence that First Nations lived on the island for several thousand years pre-contact, but few of their names persist. The cultural and economic hub is Ganges on the harbour of the same name. It was formerly called Admiralty Bay, but later changed to recognize the flagship of the Royal Navy's Pacific Station, HMS *Ganges*.

This ship was commanded by Captain John Fulford, who is honoured in the names of the village and harbour on the south end of the island that serve as a terminal for BC Ferries service to Swartz Bay. There is a Tsawout First Nation reserve on the right side as the ferry enters the harbour, at the site of an old village.

There are also ferry terminals at Long Harbour, with service to Tsawwassen and the other Gulf Islands, and at Vesuvius, with service to Crofton on Vancouver Island.

Few people are aware that in the late nineteenth century Salt Spring Island was a leading producer of apples in British Columbia. In 1894, apple trees outnumbered people ten to one. One of the orchards was at Ruckle Farm, which is now a provincial park, and visible from the ferry at Beaver

SALT SPRING ISLAND ARCHIVES

Point. By the time World War I erupted the Okanagan Valley had surpassed Salt Spring's production. Today, many specialty orchards survive, producing some 350 varieties of organic apples, and islanders celebrate their apple-growing heritage at an annual festival.

Maple Bay

First Nations on the BC coast had a long tradition of travelling in their dugout canoes, to trade, visit, take slaves and sometimes make war. In about 1860, a large band of Kwakwaka'wakw-speaking northerners travelled to Xwtl'epn'ts (Maple Bay) on a raid. The southern nations joined forces and defeated the invaders in what was the last major battle between coastal First Nations. Today, First Nations often travel together on ceremonial journeys in their traditional canoes, and gather for friendly competition in sleek, narrow racing canoes.

IMAGE H-04742 COURTESY OF ROYAL BC MUSEUM, BC ARCHIVES

The *Howe Sound Queen* eases past the pulp mill and into the dock at Crofton.

WESTERN SALT SPRING AND VANCOUVER ISLAND

VESUVIUS BAY is named for a British warship that served in the Crimean War. The area was settled by black families from the United States in the 1850s.

Salt Spring's communities are linked by winding rural roads that attract cyclists. With many travel alternatives, Salt Spring invites further exploration.

CROFTON was established by Henry Croft as the site of a smelter built to process copper ore from the nearby Lenora Mine. When the copper ran out, Crofton was left without an economic base until a pulp and paper mill was built in 1958, which remains the mainstay of the town's economy today.

The Cowichan River, a BC Heritage River, drains Cowichan Lake and the rest of the valley, reaching the sea at **COWICHAN BAY**. The estuary is listed as an Important Bird Area for the wintering and migratory birds it supports. The Cowichan people have a long history in the valley, and their oral history includes many reports of Sasquatch sightings in the area (see page 24.) Today the village of Cowichan Bay features an active fishing fleet, and the South Cowichan Lawn Tennis Club — the second-oldest lawn tennis club in the world (after Wimbledon.)

A SPECIAL GOVERNMENT FOR A SPECIAL PLACE

In 1974 the provincial government passed the Islands Trust Act, establishing the Islands Trust with a legislated mandate to "preserve and protect" the cultural and environmental features of the Gulf Islands. Each group of islands designated as a Local Trust Area elects Trustees to a Local Trust Committee and the Trust Council. The local governments are part of a federation that plans land use and regulates development in the trust area. The act also established the Islands Trust Fund to oversee the protection of the natural values of the Gulf Islands through land acquisition, stewardship education, and legal tools called conservation covenants.

Village Bay
Collinson
Helen
Crane Point
DEACON HILL
Payne Point
Channel
Plumper Sou
Hope Bay
NORTH PENDER ISLAND
MT. MENZIES
McIntyre Point
Razor Poin
Bay
Port Browning
CRAMER HILL
Shark Cove
MT. NORMAN
Shingle Bay
Pender Lake
Bedwell
Mouat Point
Thieves Bay
Boat Nook
Oaks Blu
on Channel

0   1   2
Kilometres

ISLAND
REGINALD HILL
Parkin Point
Reynard Point
Moresby Island
Canoe Rock
Fulford Harbour
Eleanor Point
Turnbull Reef
Pellow Islets
Seymour Point
Russel Island
Chads Island
Portland Island
Prevost Passage
Kanaka Point
Tortoise Islets
Brethour Island
Brackman Island
Hood Island
Moresby Passage
Fulford Harbour
Isabella Point
Shute Passage
Sheep Island
Isabella Island
Domville Island
Knapp Island
Pym Island
Piers Island
Fir Cone Point
Charmer Point
Wilhelm Point
Coal Island
MT. TUAM
Goudge Island
Kamai Point
Forrest Island
Colburne Passage
Sidney
CHANNEL
Swartz Bay Terminal
Fernie Island
Cape Keppel
Tsehum Harbour
Armstrong Point
Ker Island
Roberts Bay
Roberts Point
NORTH SAANICH
Deep Cove
Sidney
SAANICH INLE
Patricia Bay
Bazan Bay
AREA SHOWN

Sunset from Portland Island

PORTLAND ISLAND

Portland Island was called SXECOTEN in the SENCOTEN dialect — "dry mouth." The island was settled in the 1880s by Hawaiian immigrants called Kanakas. One owner raised race horses on the island and even built a racetrack there. No longer occupied, the island was given by the province to Princess Margaret in 1958, but later returned to British Columbia as a Provincial Marine Park. It is now part of the Gulf Islands National Park Reserve. British Columbia's first underwater artificial reef was created with the intentional sinking of the *G.B. Church* off the island's southeast tip.

RUSSELL ISLAND

This small island at the mouth of Fulford Harbour was settled by Kanakas, and visited by First Nations people.

PIERS ISLAND

From 1932 to 1936, Piers Island was designated as a penal colony to house Doukhobors, who were convicted of crimes committed in the name of their religious beliefs. When the colony closed, lumber was

William Naukana, a Kanaka, is believed to be of Hawaiian royal descent.

SALT SPRING ISLAND ARCHIVES

salvaged for the old Hope Bay store on Pender Island. The island is now a residential area and only emergency vehicles are allowed, so many properties have private docks that are visible from the ferry.

MORESBY ISLAND is privately owned and has a dairy farm at the north end.

On the rocky knolls and promontories of southern Vancouver Island and the Gulf Islands, small trees, gnarled and twisted, eke out a living in the dry summers. These are Garry Oaks, British Columbia's only representative of this family. In the US, the species is called Oregon White Oak. In deeper soils, the oaks grow to become stately trees, the last of which can be found in many parts of greater Victoria.

There are very few places left where these older trees are growing in intact ecosystems, with younger trees coming along to replace them. With its unique association of plants, the Garry Oak ecosystem is one of the rarest in Canada, with only about one per cent still left intact. April brings a breathtaking display of wildflowers, with White Fawn Lilies, and blue Common Camas erupting in broad drifts across the Garry Oak meadows.

Natural fires played an important role in the Garry Oak ecosystem. While they scorched the grass and shrub layer, they were not hot enough to kill the trees. First Nations people used fire too, as they managed the meadows to maintain a steady harvest of camas bulbs to sustain them through the winters. This ancient practice has recently been revived on some traditional harvesting sites.

A Diverse and Fragile Landscape

Canada's Gulf Islands, along with the southern and eastern shores of Vancouver Island, are home to an ecosystem known as the Coastal Douglas-Fir biogeoclimatic zone. It's a place where a unique combination of geography and climate combine to produce an incredible diversity of plants and animals. This ecosystem has evolved since the end of the last ice age, but today less than one per cent of the habitat remains in its natural state, and many species are threatened.

GREEN AND GROWING

Douglas-Fir

Douglas-Fir is not a fir at all and its cones, hanging down from the branches, are obviously different from the upright cones of the true firs. Historical records document specimens that were probably over 120 metres tall, but trees over 90 metres are rare today, a testament to their desirability as a provider of lumber. Canada's largest living thing is believed to be the Red Creek Fir, a giant with a broken top that stands near Port Renfrew on Vancouver Island, its 1,000-year life recognized only by a fading, handmade sign.

Lying in the dry rain shadow of the Olympic and Vancouver Island Mountains, the Douglas-Fir ecosystem stretches from the southern tip of Vancouver Island up the east coast as far as about Campbell River. Here, the Douglas-Fir is a "climax species," for there is insufficient moisture in most areas to support the cedar and hemlock that would normally replace it. Openings in the forest support Broadleaf Maples, western cousins of a familiar family, with leaves as large as dinner plates. On drier sites, Arbutus finds a home where the Douglas-Firs cannot crowd it out (see page 9).

Calypso Orchid

The forest ecosystem is more than just a collection of species. Some of these species are inextricably bound to each other. The lovely Calypso Orchid, for example, grows only in association with conifer trees on the West Coast. It uses nutrients from the mycelium, or underground portion,

strength. After being worked to increase their suppleness, the withes were often used to fasten tools to handles.

The most important product made from cedar may have been the remarkably seaworthy dugout canoes. All coastal First Nations people carved these canoes, and some also traded canoes for other goods. Voyages of thousands of kilometres were not unusual.

The light and workable wood of Western Redcedar was also used in the carving of totems and other figures. In the Salish Sea, "welcoming figures" with hands upraised were more commonly carved rather than totems.

Western Redcedar splits easily and is light and resistant to rot — all traits that have endeared it to European settlers too. Trees that are spared the chain saw may live more than 1,000 years. The tops of older trees often die off, leaving silvery spires to mark their presence in the forest.

Yellow Cedar is closely related to Western Redcedar but is a cypress. Around the Strait of Georgia it grows at higher elevation. Its wood is creamy white and valued by carvers and boatbuilders. It has a pungent aroma.

Pacific Dogwood

Every May, forest openings and edges are touched with a display of creamy white blooms courtesy of the Pacific Dogwood. The tree manages quite well in shaded areas, but comes into its glory in the open, often in a residential area. Here the tree takes a more rounded shape and may be completely white in spring.

The blossoms we see are in fact modified leaf bracts that turn white, looking like flower petals. The true flowers are nondescript, clustered at the centre of the white foliage. They are followed at summer's end by reddish berry-like

of a fungus that in turn gets its nutrients from the roots of the conifers. Even the germination of the orchid's seed is dependent on this crucial relationship. It's not surprising that these captivating forest dwellers are difficult to transplant.

Western Redcedar

Common names for plants and animals are often deceiving. This tree is not a cedar at all — that distinction belongs to the Cedar of Lebanon and its cousins we see as garden specimens. Western Redcedar is a member of a family called arborvitae, a word which translates as "tree of life." For the first people of the West Coast, it was exactly that — a resource that provided a wealth of material to sustain life.

First Nations people harvested the shaggy bark of this species in strips from younger living trees without killing the tree. Bark was separated into inner and outer layers, and treated carefully to suit various applications. Finer fibres were used in soft clothing that could be made water repellant. Coarser layers were woven into mats and baskets, and plaited into coils of sturdy rope. Slim curving lower branches called "withes" were valued for their

Most puffins in British Columbia nest on isolated offshore islets, and only a few are seen each year by lucky observers in the southern Strait of Georgia. These birds are alcids, seabirds that swim underwater using their wings instead of their feet. Their brightly coloured bill sheaths are acquired prior to the breeding season, and drop off in the early fall, leaving a much plainer bird to spend the winter in offshore waters. Puffin bills were valued as a kind of currency and as raw materials for rattles and adornment by many First Nations. Tufted Puffins have nested on Mandarte Island in the past and are most likely to be seen in waters near Swartz Bay.

drupes that are a favourite food of Band-Tailed Pigeons. A little later, the colour of the leaves changes to a blend of reds, from rosy pink to reddish purple, a welcome accent in the monochromatic western forest.

The wood from all dogwood species has been used for a variety of implements requiring hardness and durability: golf club heads, piano keys and bobbins and shuttles on textile machinery.

The Pacific Dogwood has been British Columbia's floral emblem since 1956, and although it is protected under many municipal tree bylaws, it is not protected by any provincial legislation.

ON WESTERN WINGS

Glaucous-Winged Gull

Gulls are the most common birds seen along the British Columbia coast. Many species occur here, but the Glaucous-Winged is probably the most familiar. Its name means "pale-winged" — a reference to the colour of its wingtips, which are grey like its mantle, or back. It is a resident along the coast, nesting primarily in colonies on rocky islets offshore.

Gulls are opportunistic feeders. When tides are low, they feed on marine life, often dropping clams to break them open on the rocks. They also follow farm machinery, to feed on small mammals and invertebrates. This species frequently hybridizes with the much darker Western Gull. There are many individuals that are intermediate in colour, especially in the southern Strait of Georgia, giving birders some challenging identification problems.

Pigeon Guillemot

The Pigeon Guillemot is another alcid, using its wings to "fly" underwater. Black with white wing patches and brilliant red feet, they're hard to miss. These birds nest on cliff ledges and in rocky crevices. Some have found the girders around ferry docks to be a satisfactory substitute for a nesting site.

Pacific Loon

There are five species of loons that nest in North America. This loon was once known as the Arctic Loon, but that species was split in two. The Siberian population retained the old species name, but the majority of the North American breeders became known as Pacific Loons. This species migrates north in April and May, often gathering in large flocks to feed along the way. Active Pass is an important fuelling stop on the West Coast. In the spring, look for silvery-grey heads on low-riding bodies in the water. Wintering birds are more drab, slate-coloured above and whiter below. Their calls are similar to the familiar wails and yodels of the larger and more solitary Common Loon, which occurs on our coast mostly in dull winter plumage.

Cormorants

There are three species of cormorants on the coast. All are primitive-looking birds, but they are well-adapted to a life in the water. They make their living by diving for small fish, so it is important that they are not too buoyant. Unlike most waterbirds, cormorants do not rely on body oils to waterproof their feathers, which decreases their buoyancy and allows them to dive deeper. The downside is that they must dry their feathers when they come out of the water, by holding their wings away from their bodies.

The smallest is the Pelagic Cormorant, which is easy to identify in spring with its white leggings. Double-crested Cormorants are the largest, and usually have some yellow at the base of the bill in any season. Brandt's Cormorants fall in the middle; it's safest to identify them in the spring by their fine white neck plumes.

Scoters

Scoters are sea ducks that are commonly seen in "rafts" from fall through spring. Male Surf Scoters have gaudy heads and bills, and are sometimes mistaken for puffins. White-Winged Scoters are less brightly marked. In spring, they move north and east to nest near fresh water.

Black Turnstone

Look for these white-bellied dark birds foraging among the marine animals on dock pilings and beaches. The ferry dock at Tsawwassen is often a good place during the winter months. By May, all the Black Turnstones have gone north to breed on the Bering Sea shores of Alaska. The frenzy of Arctic breeding is finished by early July, and the turnstones fly to friendlier shores for the winter. They flock together for increased security, and when danger threatens, all the birds flush, exposing dramatic black and white wings. It may startle a predator just long enough for the birds to elude capture.

Black Oystercatcher

The rocky shorelines of the southern Strait of Georgia are home to a small but stable population of Black Oystercatchers. These striking birds are difficult to see on the rocks, but announce themselves with piercing cries. Oystercatchers are non-migratory, spending the winter in small social flocks, and pairing up in the spring to nest. The nest is little more than a few bits of shell gathered just above the high tide line on a rugged islet or promontory. Two or three chicks leave the nest hours after hatching, and rely on the warning calls of their parents and camouflage to avoid predators.

Steller's Jay

British Columbia's provincial bird is the bright and brash Steller's Jay. The brilliant blues in its plumage are the result not of feather pigments, but blue light reflected by the feather structure. Like all members of the crow family, these jays are intelligent and good mimics; some imitate the calls of the Red-Tailed Hawk to help defend their territories. Steller's Jays prefer coniferous forests, but often venture into more settled areas during the leaner winter months. Their diet includes a variety of plant and animal life, including the eggs and nestlings of other birds. They are fond of Garry Oak acorns, many of which are buried. Some of these are never recovered, and may become young oak trees — an important link in the sustainability of a threatened tree species.

Band-Tailed Pigeon

The familiar flocks of pigeons in our city parks and urban centres are Rock Pigeons, introduced by European settlers to North America. British Columbia also has a native pigeon that reaches the northern limit of its range in the southwestern quarter of the province. The Band-Tailed Pigeon looks similar to its cousin, but is slightly larger, and shuns densely populated areas in favour of coniferous forests, where flocks may be seen racing across the sky. These graceful and speedy migrants winter to the south of British Columbia, arriving in the spring to build their flimsy stick nests.

Like other pigeons, Band-Tailed Pigeons feed their young a regurgitated mash known as "pigeon milk." Later in the summer and fall, they move to more open woodlands and suburban areas to feed on Garry Oak acorns and the fruits of Arbutus and Pacific Dogwood trees. Occasionally flocks of 1,000 or more are seen foraging on harvested agricultural fields. Formerly in serious decline because of hunting, the species is listed as being of "special concern" by the Committee on the Status of Endangered Wildlife in Canada (COSEWIC).

Salish Sea Mammals

Dall's Porpoise

It's difficult to get a good look at Dall's Porpoises. The speedy mammals travel in small groups that scarcely break the surface to breathe. They are sometimes confused with the much larger Killer Whale because of their black and white colour markings.

Harbour Porpoises may also be seen; they are smaller and less aggressive swimmers.

Pacific White-Sided Dolphins

Like Humpback Whales, Pacific White-Sided Dolphins raise eyebrows these days if they are seen in the southern Strait of Georgia. Unlike the whales though, these acrobatic mammals were not persecuted in the past, so their return to these waters may be a reflection of changing temperatures or prey availability. White-Sides usually travel in groups, with numbers in the hundreds not uncommon. They are fast, agile and often approach boats to play in the bow wave and wake. They frequently jump clear of the water, unlike porpoises. It's thought that the small local population may go offshore in the winter. There are infrequent sightings in the Gulf Islands, but researchers feel this may change, so watch for them to add some excitement to your ferry trip.

Humpback Whale

In the early 1900s, there was a population of Humpback Whales that frequented the southern Strait of Georgia. As industrial whaling depleted the more abundant offshore stocks, efforts were redirected at smaller populations. In 1907, a whaling station opened near Nanaimo, but only operated for one season. The whalers took the entire population of Humpbacks from nearby waters. Today, Humpback Whales are returning in numbers to British Columbia's central coast, Haida Gwaii, and northern Vancouver Island waters. Sightings have increased encouragingly in the southern Strait of Georgia, and a recovery looks promising.

Humpback Whales are mid-sized baleen whales, which feed by filtering small marine organisms through a fringe of horny baleen plates hanging from their upper jaws. Females can weigh up to 35 tonnes and reach 15 metres in length. Males are slightly smaller. Feeding dives may last from a few seconds to ten minutes, depending on the depth of the food source. Deeper dives are indicated when a whale shows its tail

A Humpback Whale's tail fluke appears as it begins a deep dive.

fluke before it goes down. Humpbacks have very long pectoral fins, which they sometimes slap on the water. They are very demonstrative, and "breach" more than other species.

Where the Land Meets the Sea

A ferry ride through the Gulf Islands carries us through a wonderfully diverse terrestrial world, but beneath the ship's hull lies an equally diverse ecosystem we cannot see — the marine world. With a little care, we can catch glimpses of this other domain.

Twice daily, the gravitational pull of the moon and the sun forces the Salish Sea to rise and fall in what we know as high and low tides. The height of the tides varies through the month, but in this area, it may be three to four metres. When the tide is out, travellers can sometimes see marine life exposed on the rocks and beaches.

Rockweed and Bull Kelp

Rockweed is one of the marine algae — not a flowering plant. It has distinctive air bladders that keep it buoyant. Rockweed often carpets the rocks of the intertidal zone, looking like a band of olive brown at a distance. Sometimes it is torn away from the rocks by waves, and forms floating mats, often with the long brown "stipes" or stems of a large marine alga called Bull Kelp. There are many species of kelp, but this one is very common. It creates underwater forests that provide cover for juvenile fish and other marine life. It is an annual, growing up to 60 centimetres a day, which makes it the fastest-growing and largest seaweed in the world.

Ochre Stars

Even at a distance, splashes of bright orange, red and purple can sometimes be seen along the shore at low tide or in the shallows at some ferry docks. These are all different colour forms of the Ochre Star, one of many species of sea stars in the Salish Sea. Sea stars are very variable. This species has a rough outer surface, while others are soft or slippery. Ochre Stars have five arms, and if one is lost, another will grow to replace it. Sea stars move using a hydraulic system to power their small suction feet. They eat a variety of marine animals, including crabs, mollusks, and other sea stars. Glaucous-Wiinged Gulls forage in the intertidal zone regularly, and it is not uncommon to see one with a half-swallowed sea star.

WHAT DOES THE FUTURE HOLD?

Our planet is facing dramatic consequences because of worldwide climate change. Each region must deal with different challenges. In the Gulf Islands, it is expected that the threatened Garry Oak ecosystem may actually benefit from warmer summers, but some species, like Western Redcedar, are already showing signs of stress. The marine environment has seen unprecedented changes. The pressures of population growth, resource extraction and environmental pollutants all put additional strain on some of Canada's most vulnerable species.

Fortunately there are many government and non-government agencies working to protect threatened habitats and species, but it's a major challenge. The good news is that increasing protected areas also increases carbon storage, a critical component in the fight against climate change.

Environmental stewardship though, is not just for some places, not just for some species and not just for some people to practise. The task is daunting but every task is a series of small steps, and every small step each of us takes brings us closer to the goal.